FROM

TO I'M

Discover Your Life's Purpose
And Monetize It

By
Jola Pypno-Crapanzano

Dedicated to

My Husband Bill and
My Children Nicolette and Christopher

"Live your life to
the fullest
every day
before you
run out of time"
- Jola Pypno-Crapanzano

Table of Contents

Introduction
My Story And How It Impacted
My Life's Purpose

"The moment you decide that
you're meant for bigger things,
everything changes."

Our life stories are unique, and they shape not only who we are but also help determine our purpose in life. I am pleased to share my personal story based on a potent exercise called "10 Picture timeline", which I learned from my mentor Joel Bauer. This exercise was one of the hardest things I have ever done but also the most rewarding. The objective was to pick only ten pictures representing important events and pivotal moments in my life. Then, based on them, I determined the phases I went through, the critical lessons I have learned, and how they impacted my life.

Having hundreds of thousands of pictures, it seemed mission impossible even to imagine how can I do it. But after some serious thinking and narrowing it down, I was able to pick ten images that created a powerful timeline, and I was able to pinpoint invaluable life lessons.

My story starts with growing up and being raised in Poland by two incredible parents, my mom Maria, and my dad Marian, who dedicated their lives to me and my brother Wojtek.

My mom had a massive influence on my life at this age; she was a powerful, very loving woman who gave everything she got to us, saving nothing for herself. I learned from this phase that as a parent, I could give my children a lot, but I must keep a little bit of myself for myself and have time for my hobbies and things I love. My dad also loved and supported us unconditionally, and he always accepted 100% of the decisions we made.

Growing up in a very depressed economy, I became exposed to a scarcity mindset and limiting beliefs at a very young age. I learned from that time that your circumstances don't determine your outcomes. Having very few material possessions in my early years massively boosted my creativity. I played with sticks building imaginary houses; I designed my original pieces of clothing and decorated spaces with unusual items. In school, we didn't have the modern means the kids in western countries had, but it didn't stop me from becoming one of the top students in my class in all grades. It is not our lack of resources but how resourceful we can get that matters.

At this time, I developed my big passion and love for travel. I wanted to visit exotic places around the world more than anything else. But unfortunately, my parents couldn't afford it, and we could only travel domestically.

It was during college that my dreams came true. I became a licensed tour guide and began traveling around the globe. Looking back, I was able to manifest it because I prepared; I studied foreign languages: English, German and Russian. Intuitively, I knew it would help me open the path to seeing the world. I wanted it so badly and believed I could figure out how to do it.

I graduated college with a master's degree in Scientific-Technical Information, including Computer Science, but my heart wasn't in it. Instead, I chose to follow my passion for travel. And even when I received an offer to continue my education and earn Ph.D., it didn't change my mind. On the contrary, it was the first time I followed my dreams and felt truly happy. That was a powerful life lesson - always choose happiness.

The next crucial phase was my move to the United States. Looking back, it is one of the biggest acts of courage I've ever demonstrated. Life in the USA offered many opportunities, and incredible doors opened. But it didn't happen at no cost. It required sacrifices, like leaving my family and everything I knew behind and starting from scratch. But another lesson was already developing – my new life in New York City, because as they say if you can make it here, you can make it anywhere. After a very short time, I was able to buy my first car and condo with a gorgeous view of Manhattan, and I could continue traveling. Life was perfect.

The next phase was meeting the love of my life and my future husband. We have been married for 26 years, constantly growing as a couple, and our commitment to each other is getting stronger. We don't just buy houses; we build homes. We raise a family. We are now proud parents of two exceptional children: Nicolette and Chris.

And that's the next phase of my life -becoming a mother. Having my children in my arms and on my lap was one of the happiest and truly blissful moments. And the important thing is, it was a miracle. My children proved that dreams come true and that miracles are possible. The likelihood of me becoming pregnant was very tiny due to the removal of the cysts from my ovaries which damaged them. But it happened, and the lesson learned here was: Never give up hope.

Maybe because it was such a blessing to have my babies, I decided to spoil them rotten and create abundance for them; I never experienced myself as a child. I taught them the Polish language and traditions and ensured they knew their roots. My parents visited us every year, and they could communicate with them easily. Following my dad's example, I also support my children in pursuing their dreams and passions: dance for my daughter and lacrosse for my son.

My parents' deaths were the most challenging times of my life. I loved them more than words describe. Losing them was a wake-up call and made me realize my health's importance. Coincidentally, my metabolism slowed down, and I put some weight on. I knew I had to change my lifestyle, and I did. I underwent a significant transformation. Practicing portion-controlled nutrition and regular workouts, I lost 38 pounds in five months. More importantly, I kept it off. I inspired many people and started teaching them my process. Subsequentially, I became a fitness and wellness coach. That started a chain of reactions. I met my first mentor Brendon Burchard, and ultimately became a Certified High Performance Coach.

My personal development journey continues, I am clear on what I want to achieve and who I want to become, and I continue working on my energy and vitality. I am much bolder and more courageous; I am super productive and a master implementor. I am much more influential, which helped me build my coaching business. I invested a lot of time and money in my personal growth, got multiple certifications, and now I am monetizing my life experience with multiple strings of income.

It was only possible because I followed my heart once again. A few years ago, my life looked picture-perfect, but something was missing. I wasn't feeling fulfilled and realized I wasn't creating a lasting legacy for my children. I wanted to live life with no regrets, on my terms, and pass what I've learned forward. That's how the Coaching journey with Jola, LLC, was born, and my Exceptional Life Academy 2.0 membership followed. I am on a mission to impact millions of lives, be the most extraordinary mentor, author, coach, and speaker, and help others define, design, and deliver a life of fulfillment, joy, and purpose.

> **"You're amazing, unique, one of a kind. Don't ruin this masterpiece by copying others.".**

1

Rise Of A Super-Human

"When your desires are strong enough you will appear to possess superhuman powers to achieve"

- Napoleon Hill

Ever since I remember, I have been fascinated by people who possess extraordinary talents, gifts, and powers. I admired fabulous athletes constantly improving their skills and beating world and Olympic records. I greatly appreciated terrific artists who created inspiring music, dance, painting, sculpture, literature, and design pieces. I was in awe of wickedly smart scientists and innovators whose brilliant work and ideas made our lives better and more convenient. Influential businesspeople who created unbelievable biz empires and became multi-millionaires and billionaires inspired me. I studied brilliant thought leaders and mentors whose teachings attracted and influenced masses worldwide to listen to them, learn from them, and follow them. And finally, I paid close attention to people gifted with unusual, almost unnatural skills, the lightworkers, energy healers, fortune tellers, mediums, shamans, and intuitive who accomplished miraculous things.

In recent years I immersed myself in studying the brilliant minds of very successful, high achievers who were able to succeed in their area of genius and lived to the fullest in all other areas of their lives. I was particularly interested in people who could crack the code of optimizing and maximizing their time, space, resources, and talents to create extraordinary results and live great lives.

What I found out was quite surprising to me; even though they rarely talked about it, most of the highest performers were aware of and closely followed the Universal Laws and tuned into the Universal energy and intelligence. They knew how to raise their vibration to attract and achieve what they desired. They knew how to optimize their bodies, minds, and spirits. They figured out how to become great experts in one area without sacrificing others by tending to and caring for their physical, mental, and spiritual energy. They followed their intuition and knew how to get into a state of flow.

What once was considered woo-woo became the unspoken norm for people achieving lasting success. What differentiates them from the rest is their level of consciousness. The modern-age geniuses show that their phenomenon lies in following certain rituals and doing certain things daily to become the best versions of themselves. They make conscious choices to achieve something, let go of the fear, trust, and surrender, take inspired, sometimes uncomfortable action, and then let the Universe do its work, and in effect, reality changes to help them.

To become new-age super-human and achieve desired extraordinary levels of success and happiness, we can't outthink certain things; we must feel them, connect to nature, and be more in the present moment.

We must back up our talent and brilliant ideas with intuition, trust, and massive, inspired action. We must find the golden middle between the masculine energy of the rigid strategies and the feminine energy of the flow.

My objective is to live my life to the fullest, on my terms, without regrets - Life by design, not in default, I am a student of life, and in this book "From IMPOSSIBLE to I'M POSSIBLE" I share with you what I have learned.

"Superhuman effort isn't worth a damn unless it achieves results."

~ Ernest Shackleton

2

The Inner Game Of Happiness - How To Live An Authentic Life

"An exceptional life isn't the result of lucky breaks, but excellent choices."

-Robin Sharma

According to some of its definitions, happiness is the mental or emotional state of well-being characterized by pleasant emotions. However, it is more than just a positive mood; it's a state of well-being with a sense of meaning and deep contentment.

We all want to be happier, but only a few know how to improve our happiness. Here are a few things that most people think will make them happier: a great relationship, a job that better provides for them and their family, more flexibility at work, a bigger house, having a baby, looking younger, being healthier, losing weight, having more supportive parents, more money, and more time. But surprisingly, none of these things will make us substantially more comfortable. So, we tend to look for happiness in the wrong places.

Happiness is the number one goal for most people in life, it's what they constantly chase, but they have no clue how happiness works.

Happy people aren't Satisfied and excited because they have more money, fancy cars, and better looks than the less happy ones. The difference lies in their behavior; they do more things that boost their happiness. For example, they spend time with their loved ones, practice optimism, move their bodies regularly, savor life's pleasures, live in the present moment, and express gratitude for what they already have and achieved. Research shows that people rate happiness more important than other desirable outcomes, such as obtaining wealth, acquiring material goods, and even getting into heaven.

Here is some science behind happiness. According to Carl Jung, some fundamental happiness factors include good physical and mental health, good personal and intimate relationships, reasonable standards of living and satisfactory work, and the faculty for perceiving beauty in art and nature.

Harvard Medical School studies show that happiness has little to do with age and lowering stress levels; however, having a positive outlook and relaxation techniques can significantly reduce health problems and promote happiness. Other elements that increase happiness are exercise, socially interacting, and a minimum of 7 hours of sleep per night.

According to Forbes, things that can significantly improve happiness are doing good things for others, cherishing meaningful close relationships, being a contributor, doing something we are good at, and finally, taking care of ourselves in health, well-being, financial security, and work-life balance.

And even though half of our happiness levels depend on our genes (some people are predisposed to be happier), it doesn't mean we can't improve our overall happiness.

Research shows that 40% of happiness comes from our choices, and only 10% depends on circumstances. And that's fantastic news because we can't change our genes, and often we can't change our circumstances, but we can change how we think. So don't sweat the small stuff; focus on what's important, let go of past failures, and pay attention to what makes you happy now.

Happiness is a decision. Decide today!

"Happiness will be fleeting if you constantly search for it in places that can be taken away. It's an inside job."

-Nikki Rowe

3

An Empty
Rice Bowl

*"Never break another
man's rice bowl"*

- Akio Morita

I am a student of life, constantly thirsty for new knowledge like a sponge. I can learn something fascinating and new daily: a powerful insight, a nugget of wisdom, a practical tip, an exciting fact, etc.

I recently learned a concept of an Empty Rice Bowl, which beautifully illustrates "the beginner's mind." It comes from an old story from the Zen Buddhist tradition.

The very abbreviated version of this story goes like this: Once upon a time, a very knowledgeable scholar lived. He heard of a Zen Buddhist master, one of the wisest people in the land, and he developed a deep desire to study under the master. So, he traveled for days to reach him. When he finally arrived at the secluded location where the master resided, he realized that even though he was very famous and accomplished, the master knew nothing about him. So, the master invited him to share a meal. During the dinner, the scholar immediately introduced himself and pointed out his accomplishments. While he talked, the master kept filling up his bowl with rice. The scholar kept talking and talking until he noticed the rice overflowing the bowl. He asked the master why he kept putting more and more rice in his bowl. And the master replied: "Your mind is like this rice bowl. It is so full of knowledge that nothing else will fit. For me to teach you wisdom, you must first empty your mind."

In essence, learning a pearl of new wisdom is impossible if there is no room for new teachings. It also implies that you are teachable if you know that you don't know.

Many people are afraid to be seen as beginners or to admit that they don't know something. They don't want others to assume that they must be stupid if they don't know something. I am a beginner in almost everything related to my recent journey into consciousness and enlightenment. But I'm not afraid or ashamed to admit it. On the contrary, I am delighted and proud that I discovered this path; some people live their entire lives and never do.

Another thing that people are afraid of is being seen starting small, regardless of what it is they're doing. I could be starting their business, hobby, or anything. They think that if they don't have everything figured out perfectly, it's better not to start. They often compare their beginning with someone else's middle or end, and it causes them to feel insecure, paralyzes their action, or worse, causes no action at all. The fear of judgment and the comparison game kills their creativity, original approach, and innovative thinking.

Always have an empty rice bowl.

"To empty the rice bowl is to become receptive to the wisdom and guidance of the Universe. The tricky part is to let go of the belief that we must *think up some solution.* We must become skillful in expanding the empty mind so that it may function as something like a receiver so the solution can be downloaded!"

4

The Importance
Of
Discovering Your Purpose

*"Purpose isn't a concept that you
have; it's something you are enacting,
something you ultimately define,
not find"*

– *Brendon Burchard*

The definition of purpose states that it is the reason something is done or created or exists. To psychologists, the purpose is an abiding intention to achieve a long-term goal that is both personally meaningful and makes a positive mark on the world. Defining purpose is one of the essential activities in personal development.

Like happiness, the purpose is not a destination but a journey and practice. The challenge is that we can have different purposes in different areas of our life as well as at other times of our life. Some people live their entire lives trying to figure out the purpose of their existence.

When you know your life's purpose, you tend to live a more meaningful existence than those who don't. You tend to live each day to the fullest because you know who you are, where you're coming from, and where you're going.

"Having a purpose is the difference between making a living and making a life".

– Tom Thiss

There are several benefits of discovering your purpose in life:

1. You will gain clarity in your life. Clarity is power; therefore, knowing your purpose in life will make you unstoppable. You will see what you want and won't waste your time on meaningless things.

2. You will live a life based on your most important values. These values will guide your decisions in life and help define your goals, and help you connect with others who share a similar way of viewing the world.

3. You will stay focused and avoid distractions. It will become easier for you to focus on what matters the most in your life. You will be able to find direction and stay away from distractions.

4. You will live with congruence and integrity. You will know who you are, what you are, and why you are, and live true to your core values.

5. You will be passionate about your goals. This passion will drive you to achieve extraordinary things in life and reach your personal and professional goals.

6. You will find flow in life. Knowing your true purpose will help you connect to the universal stream of consciousness. You will let things happen instead of fighting against them.

7. You will become more courageous. Your purpose and strong why will help you battle your fears.

8. You will have more trust. Knowing your true purpose will encourage synchronicities and serendipities in your life, and you will develop more trust and faith in other people.

9. You will make a more significant impact through your work and will feel more gratified.

10. You will have more fun in life. Knowing your purpose in life, you will enjoy every minute of it and become more creative.

There are countless other benefits of knowing your purpose, such as:

- increased optimism,
- resiliency,
- hope,
- joy
- happiness, and
- satisfaction

- better physical, mental, and emotional health,
- lower risk of death,
- engagement,
- sense of belonging,
- career satisfaction,
- higher income.

When you maximize your talents, you are on the path, on purpose, and target. When you hear yourself say: I am stressed; I'm going to have a breakdown, you are not on your path, and you're most likely not doing what you are here to do.

How Can We Discover Our Purpose

"Your purpose in life is to find your purpose and give your whole heart and soul to it."

-Buddha

One of the very well-known methods is IKIGAI (the intrinsic value and worth that the person finds in their life)- the Japanese art of unlocking your best life, relieving anxiety, and discovering your happiness and purpose.

The western version of IKIGAI is based on a diagram created by Spanish author Andres Zuzunaga, known as the purpose Venn Diagram. The graph represents four components of achieving IKIGAI:

1. Finding what you love
2. Finding what the world needs
3. Finding what you are good at
4. Finding what you can get paid for

These four components intersect with each other to create creative sub-goals:

1. Passion is where "what you love" intersects with "what you are good at"
2. The Mission is where "what you love" intersects with "what the world needs."
3. The Vocation is where "what the world needs" intersects with "what you can get paid for."
4. The Profession is where "what you are good at" intersects with "what you can get paid for."

According to the diagram, your IKIGAI would be the sum of what you love, what you are good at, what the world needs, and what you can get paid for.

So, make finding your purpose a priority; you will find the peace and serenity that comes from leading a purpose-driven life. Because as Wayne Dyer said: "When you stay on purpose and refuse to be discouraged by fear, you align with the infinite self, in which all possibilities exist.

**"The purpose of life is a
life of purpose."**

– Robert Byrne

5

Live A Life
Worth Living

*"Live out of your imagination,
not your history."*

-Stephen Covey

The more we raise our awareness and consciousness and educate ourselves, the more we realize the importance of living life to the fullest. A life that is engaged, joyful, confident, fulfills the most profound dreams and desires, and is congruent with them. A life that leaves no room for regrets and that produces a fantastic legacy for the future generation.

I know these are lofty words; perhaps you have heard them before. But are you living your life to the fullest? Is your life truly a masterpiece worth living?

If your answer is yes – excellent! If your answer is no, here are a few powerful ideas for changing that.

Appreciate your life every hour of every day, regardless of what you're doing. Remind yourself of a crisis, or a past traumatic experience, when you or one of your loved ones were in great danger, pain, or misery. Remember how you thought that if you survived, you'd be so grateful for your life, and you'll change to make every minute count going forward? And yes, right after that catastrophic incident passed, you felt greater joy and appreciation of every moment, but that heightened appreciation didn't last very long. Instead, it was replaced by taking your life for granted and living on autopilot again.

Be sure to create that appreciation before the crisis in your life. Feel how good it is to be alive and to have the privilege of living regardless of the circumstances. Stop living on autopilot, like a robot that repeats the same mundane tasks daily without being present. Instead, slow down, look around, smell, touch, and genuinely feel grateful for being able to do that activity and just being alive. Think what you can appreciate about your life right now: perhaps your health, your family or friends, some sensual experiences like food and drinks, a beautiful sunny day, a warm shower, a fragrant shampoo, soft, comfy clothes, new learning, and growth or opportunities and possibilities for the future that excite you.

Take a moment a write these things down and make a habit of daily gratitude journaling. You will be astounded by how your life will change for the better by simply bringing awareness of everything you are grateful for now in this extraordinarily precious life.

The Dalai Lama, when asked what surprised him most about humanity, answered:

"Man. Because he sacrifices his health in order to make money. Then he sacrifices money to recuperate his health. And then he is so anxious about the future that he does not enjoy the present; the result being that he does not live

**in the present or the future;
he lives as if he is never going to
die and then dies having never
really lived."**

Don't be that Man; live a life worth living!

6

How to gain the end-of-life perspective before your life ends?

"When your life flashes before your eyes at the end, make sure it's a good movie you're watching"

- Stewart Stafford

One of the most impactful experiences of my life was the service I used to provide as a young girl in the nursing home. I used to go there after school every week and spend time with the lonely older people who their children often abandoned. It was a very sad life lesson. These mothers, fathers, and grandparents were waiting for me like I was their family. I will never forget the joy I saw in their eyes when I accompanied them, chitchatting while sharing small meals. They were always trying to give me reasons and excuses why their kids and grandkids weren't coming to visit them. They silently suffered and had a lot of regrets and very little hope for the better.

So, at a very young age, I gained this awareness and desire to live my life so that I won't have regrets at the end of my time.

But the turning point happened much later when I came across a book, "The top five regrets of the dying" by Bronnie Ware which was inspired by her work in palliative care. Here they are summarized:

1. I wish I were courageous to live a life true to myself, not the life others expected of me. People realize how many dreams have gone unfulfilled due to their choices.

2. I wish I hadn't worked so hard. Many people deeply regret spending so much of their lives working, missing their children growing up and the companionship of their spouses.

3. I wish I'd dared to express my feelings. People settle for a mediocre existence and never become who they could become.

4. I wish I had stayed in touch with my friends. Everyone misses their friends when they are dying and regrets not giving friendships the time and effort that they deserved

5. I wish that I had let myself be happier. Happiness is a choice, but many people don't realize that their entire life.

There are many ways of gaining that end-of-life perspective before life ends. So here are, in random order, several ideas on how to live regret-free life that predicts fulfillment at the end of it:

- Choose the job that you love and will teach you the most.

- Spend as much time as possible with your kids when they are kids. They grow up so fast you won't ever get a second chance.

- Avoid toxic people and those who are energy vampires.

- Value the quiet moments and live in the present more without reminiscing and worrying about the future.

- Don't compare yourself to others; compete only with yourself.

- It is not too late, and it's not over until it's over. No matter how many mistakes you've made, remember you must only get it right once.

- Tell people how you feel, don't hide your true feelings, and use the Ho'oponopono mantra:

> **"I am sorry.**
> **Please forgive me.**
> **Thank you.**
> **I love you".**

Learn to celebrate your failures; it's not about running the perfect race. It's about getting across the finish line.

- Maintain engagement with the world. Older people who are vital continue thinking about their future, the world, the current events; they read and keep learning.

- Make your decisions based on your dreams and aspirations, and don't try to please others - claim your life.

- Don't regret your mistakes. Instead, learn from them. There is no failure; there is only feedback.

- Start pursuing your dreams today. Some day is the one day that never comes.

- Don't be afraid to do ridiculous, silly, and funny things, and make sure you laugh a lot.

- Be willing to surrender and trust because sometimes it is worth getting rid of the life you've planned to have, the life waiting for you.

- Don't speak when angry because you can't ever take back an angry word.

- As they say, when one door closes, another one opens. Some regrets we must live with; however, get out there and keep trying because there might be something better for you.

- Be afraid of being afraid, so you don't have to have the biggest regret of all – regret that you didn't try.

And finally, ask yourself: What's your greatest regret so far, and what will you change and try to achieve before you die? What would you do if you could start your life's makeover today? What if someone handed you life's golden ticket?

We all have choices; we can go on and continue living our hectic lives the same we do now, or we can do things differently and pursue what's on our mind for a while, but we keep postponing for later or abandoning altogether. However, a life of no regrets can start right now.

I will finish with my favorite phrase:

"Live your life to the fullest every day, before you run out of time"

"In every difficult situation is potential value. Believe this, then begin looking for it."

-Norman Vincent Peale

7

The Magic
Of
Imagination

Everything you can imagine is real."
-Pablo Picasso

By its definition, imagination is a creative ability to produce and simulate novel objects, peoples, and ideas in mind without any immediate input from the senses.

Almost a century ago, Albert Einstein wrote: "Your imagination is everything. It is the preview of life's coming attractions [...] imagination is more important than knowledge. Knowledge is limited, whereas imagination embraces the entire world, stimulating progress, giving birth to evolution."

Indeed, the land of imagination is where the best ideas are born. But, unfortunately, thinking hard doesn't produce the best results and ideas. Quite the opposite; the harder you think about a specific issue or a problem, the less likely you are to come up with the solution.

So counterintuitively, instead of trying to figure out something by thinking hard, drop into your body, create stillness, and empty your mind. This technique will surprise you by generating ideas and solutions unavailable to you through hard thinking.

The following reasons block your imaginative faculties: moving too fast, thinking obsessively, holding limiting beliefs, not getting enough rest, and depleting energy reserves. They produce physical and mental tension, and everything rigid and tense can easily break. "Trying" to use your imagination will work against you as trying creates tension. Instead, be playful, curious, and explore like a fascinated anthropologist.

There are several methods to enhance imagination, but relaxing the body is the untold secret to tapping into it. One of the simplest and most effective ways to do so is by closing your eyes, taking a few slow, steady, deep breaths, and letting go of trying to control what might happen next.

Other ways to boost your imagination are: sleeping longer and taking more naps, slowing down and spending more time alone in stillness, having stimulating conversations with a variety of people, keeping an idea journal and writing freely about anything, doodling, working in a new environment, following daily ritual, exercising and meditating, listening to favorite music, taking a bath, going for a walk, playing improv games, taking pictures, doing something that produces adrenaline rush, playing with animals, hanging out with friends, doing nothing, reading creative literature, planning an ideal trip and many more.

The more attention you give your imagination, the more it will serve you. Using your Imagination to create requires you to develop a kind of "muscle" or skill.

One of my favorite ways to do it is to ask my imagination to help solve a particular issue or problem before I sleep. I make a "request" to my subconscious, and upon awakening, I remain still, tune in and listen, and recall my dreams. Sometimes the ideas are there, and I capture them without mental editing. Sometimes it takes a day or two or a week, and suddenly I get the answers while taking a shower, jogging, or driving my car. Remember that the answers will come when you loosen your grip and stop micromanaging the Universe.

That's the magic of imagination!

> **"To bring anything into your life, imagine that it's already there."**
>
> **—Richard Bach**

8

From Woo-Woo
To WOW!

*"You get in life what you have
the courage to ask for."*

-Oprah Winfrey

M y journey into consciousness started a couple of years ago. If someone told me in the past that I would write articles for magazines and even book chapters on new-age topics, I would never believe it because manifesting, chakras, energetic healing, and the Universal Laws were new to me.

Yes, I read the book and saw the movie "The Secret" years ago. Yes, I was always curious about coincidences, synchronicities, and other things like DeJaVu, oracle readings, affirmations, etc. Still, I never truly believed in the law of attraction and almost considered it all a Woo-Woo.

Things changed when I got introduced a couple of years ago for the first time to the energetic work. I became hyper-aware and genuinely fascinated by it - I completed many courses. I learned about chakras, Feng Shui, numerology, astrology, the power of our thoughts, and the words we use. I got certified as NLP and Time Line Therapy® practitioner, which prompted learning about Akashic records and card readings. My consciousness is different now than a few years ago, and I know that the manifestation work I currently do, and Chakra and Crystals healing will transport me to yet another level.

Studying, I realized how much more I needed to learn. The awareness that, in the past, I unknowingly manifested many different things blew my mind.

Here are some examples of the things I manifested: my amazing trips around the world (I visited close to 70 countries), my wonderful family (after surgery on my ovaries, doctors told me that I probably wouldn't be able to have babies, and yet on my honeymoon I got pregnant and today I have two amazing kids), my beautiful home and truly extraordinary life in the USA (I came to America from Poland with just two suitcases) and I could go on and on... I can only imagine what is possible if I intentionally use my knowledge!

In the last few months, I met incredible people, energy healers, light workers, and experts in different coaching modalities. It all happened because of one thing, one nudge I felt and one decision I made.

One day I received an invitation to co-author a book, "One" – your wellness guide to body, mind, and soul, and I intuitively agreed. The book became an international bestseller almost instantly, and it was just the beginning of my fantastic adventure into consciousness.

The chain of events continued. Afterward, another bestselling book, "#stayhome" was written at the beginning of the pandemic in 2020. After that, I became a contributing executive author for two magazines "Sibyl" and "Brainz." In August of 2021 landed on the covers of both of them. I also manifested a fabulous coaching retreat for women in Bali, Indonesia. And most recently, I presented in front of quite a big live audience for the first time in Los Angeles, California. Finally, I created my online membership called "Exceptional Life Academy 2.0", where I now serve my clients.

The book you are now holding is also a product of my manifestation. Long before I wrote it, I designed its cover, created a mockup, and took it everywhere. As a result, I felt the energy, gratitude, and joy as if I had already completed it. And that's one of the necessary steps for successful manifesting.

Not to mention small examples of things that manifest themselves almost daily. For instance, once I pulled a Quantum Oracle card that told me: "You may be introduced to someone who resonates with your heart, a job offer may come your way, or you may come across a book, video, or spiritual practice that is helpful in your daily life or business. New ideas, information, and exciting new connections are vibrating all around you" then, shortly after, I won a prize in an online contest and coincidentally came across profound intuitive reading by an incredible energy healer from Australia. And the list goes on and on...

I am so ready for more.

"Everything you want is out there waiting for you to ask. Everything you want also wants you. But you have to take action to get it."

—Jack Canfield

9

Bliss, Flow
And
High Performance

*"Go with the flow, follow your bliss
and make your little gems in life."*

I always knew that I was a high achiever who constantly sets big goals and reaches them but who also looks immediately for more aims to accomplish.

Even though this sounds super impressive and exciting, after deeper consideration, it creates a serious issue. For the last couple of years, I've been studying positive intelligence, specifically mental fitness. It became clear to me that one of the 10 Saboteurs - Hyper Achiever ruled my life very strongly. By taking a short assessment, you also can discover which Saboteurs are secretly impacting your life. In my case, it is this loud, obnoxious voice lying to me that my emotions get in the way of performance, that life is all about achieving and producing results, and that I am worthy as long as I am successful, and others think well of me.

I decided to learn more about it and what I found out was quite astonishing: for the Hyper-Achievers, self-validation, and self-love are all conditional - conditioned on continual performance, which metaphorically means that they reach a mountain, they celebrate for a couple of minutes, and then they immediately start looking for another mountain to climb. It is exhausting. It is pure insanity!

When we add that Hyper Achievers focus on external success, which leads to unsustainable workaholic tendencies and loss of touch with deeper emotional and relationship needs, they must be best at what they do. If they can't be outstanding, they won't bother, and finally, their self-acceptance continuously depends on the subsequent success - the conclusion was clear, I had a problem.

When I heard that most Hyper Achievers go to their grave still thinking about that one thing they didn't achieve on their list, I decided that enough is enough. So I carefully and intentionally picked my guiding clarity words: Bliss, Flow, and Ease. I desperately wanted to change my approach to life because I realized that the solid inner tendency to overachieve was conditioning all my life and that there would be a lot of resistance when I tried to change things.

Luckily, I was aware of the possibility of living life quite differently. I understood and often experienced a proper flow state when time seemed to slow down or even stop when I got immersed in my work.

Interestingly enough, it never feels like a chore, hustle, or grind; instead, it always makes me feel at ease and, more importantly, produces impressive outcomes.

So, what's the solution here? It is simple and obvious, but common sense is not a common practice as it often happens in life. To live feeling bliss, flow, and ease, we have to do what makes us happy and alive, and we will create incredible results without feeling stressed and overwhelmed.

"Bliss is when energy flows out for that work on its own, not when you push yourself to be energetic to get it done"

10

Raise Your Vibration, Change Your Life

"How you vibrate is what the universe echoes back to you in every moment."

- Panache

Let's face it, if the greatest minds of all time, the most brilliant achievers, and the highest-performing people in the world have figured this out and are doing it, there is a reason for it. But, of course, they don't talk about it often, and sometimes they never even mention it. Still, when intimately interviewed, they admit that they all intentionally raise their vibration all the time because, ultimately, it is the main reason for their extraordinary success and lasting happiness.

So, what is vibration anyway, and why does it matter?

It's not a secret that everything in this Universe exists out of energy and has a specific vibrational frequency. Your thoughts, feelings, and beliefs are energy and vibrate at their frequency. It would help if you raised your vibration to the level of the things you want; it's that simple.

When you raise your vibration with high-vibration thoughts and feelings:

- You attract positive energy from the Universe, and high vibration results.

- It makes you happier and more relaxed.

- It helps you have a more peaceful state of mind.

- It positively affects your body and your nervous system.

- It creates a balance of energy in your body.

- You release negative thoughts and energy.

- People enjoy being around you more.

- You feel better physically, and you are more energetic.

- You attract experiences that you desire.

- You manifest things a lot easier.

On the other hand, when you are vibrating lower, you are sad, angry, fearful, and resentful.

So it's not a gimmick; it's the study of quantum physics.

One dozen super-effective tips for raising your vibration:

Although a lot has been said and written about different ways of raising the vibration, and I believe it is very individual, there are some universal and 100% proven ways to increase your vibration instantly. So, before you start questioning positive energy from the Universe, try them for yourself and see how you feel.

1. As mentioned above, pay attention to the quality of your thoughts and feelings. Concentrate on high vibrational emotions like love, compassion, empathy, happiness, peace, joy, acceptance, etc. Try to bring the memories connected to them.

2. Fuel your body with high-vibration foods filled with positive life force energy like whole and unprocessed foods, organic fruits and vegetables, fiber-rich grains, legumes, healthy fats from seeds, nuts, cold-pressed oils, protein from grass-fed livestock, superfoods, and antioxidants.

3. Indulge in some self-care: get a relaxing and soothing massage, take a warm bath with essential oils or salts, meditate or do other mindfulness activities or breathwork. Just being mindful and practicing the state of consciousness will raise your vibrations.

4. Practice daily gratitude. Take time and journal every morning about everything you appreciate in your life, whether small or big; even just for 5 minutes, be thankful for all the great things you are blessed with.

5. Surround yourself with high-vibration positive people you love and care about; notice who gives you energy, makes you laugh, drains you, and takes your energy away. Put up boundaries against those people who are energy vampires.

6. Make sure you get enough sleep and rest. A solid 7 or 8 hours of sleep will make you wake

up with higher frequency and positive energy, feeling refreshed and ready to go.

7. Cleanse your surroundings from negative energy, and burn some incense, sage, palo santo, sandalwood, or certain herbs. Let their smoke float in the space; it will help raise the space's overall vibration.

8. Move your body. Physical exercise gets you out of your head and into your body. A mind-body connection is excellent for your health and raises your vibration by releasing endorphins. Regardless of what you commit to, yoga, running, hit cardio, or weights lifting. Just do it.

9. Learn or create something new. You can express your creativity in many ways: writing, drawing, painting, dancing, singing, decorating, or even cooking.

10. Declutter the space around you. Make your living and workplace peaceful and happy, allowing new energy to flow freely.

11. Spend time in nature. Rain or shine, go for a walk or jog outside daily, walk barefoot on the grass or the sand, swim in the ocean, sea, lake, or river, dance in the rain, walk in the

forest, sit on the hill overlooking the city, climb the mountain peak, etc.

12. Accept and forgive. Accepting people as they are and forgiving them for their mistakes will free you from negative low-vibration emotions such as anger, fear, shame, blame, revenge, disappointment, and apathy.

Ten powerful tools and methods to quickly raise your vibration:

- Use sound therapy. Listen to high-vibration music, singing bowls, bells, and gongs.

- Use crystal healing therapy. Surround yourself with crystals, gemstones, and minerals. Their vibrations can be tuned to your body and stimulate your energy.

- Use essential oils. Familiarize their scent with a particular activity, creating a connection in your brain. So, for example, when you use specific essential oil to relax you, then this scent in times of heightened stress and anxiety will help you elicit a relaxing state.

- Try Reiki or other forms of energy healing. These alternative therapies can help reduce anxiety, and pain, strengthen the immune system and accelerate healing, induce relaxation and raise the vibration.

- Do visualizations. They are an excellent way to focus your energy and raise your vibration. You can do it by visualizing beautiful places, pleasant memories, or something you desire or are currently grateful for.

- Say affirmations. They are another great way to raise your vibration by appreciating yourself and connecting with unconditional loving energy.

- Practice meditation. Meditation is a quick way to slow down, focus energy, and connect with your inner self. Early morning and bedtime meditation are the most effective ways to shift your vibration and keep negative emotions away.

- Feng-shui your space. This ancient study focuses on the location of items around the home or office, the flow of energy, and how the colors, shapes, and materials can influence you and your room. Your space can have a massive impact on your productivity, your mood, and your decisions. Allowing your home to be clutter-free can help your energy and mind flow freely.

- Place plants in your space. Getting some house plants is a great way to feel close to nature. Everything has an energetic field, and plants are not an exception; having plants and caring for them is a great way to raise your vibration and ground your energy.

- Laugh out loud. When you are in a good mood, your energy vibration levels are naturally higher. So, laugh often to lift your mood and raise your vibration level.

Enough said. No doubt that living on the higher frequencies helps us achieve immense success and lasting happiness, which we ultimately desire. There is a trick to it: Many people learn and understand the value of high vibrations but need to implement the methods and techniques. It is essential to follow and apply them continuously and then expect some results.

Look over the lists above and identify some things you can start doing immediately, then pick a few items to integrate into your daily routine. Next, create a set of reminders for yourself, place them so you can see them daily, and commit to taking daily action to raise your vibration.

It will change your life; it's a promise!

> **"If you want to find the secrets of the universe, think in terms of energy, frequency and vibration."**
>
> **—Nikola Tesla**

11

How To
Create Tranquility
In Your Busy Life

*"The idea of beauty is simplicity
and tranquility"*

-Johann Wolfgang von Goethe

In recent years our lives, without a shadow of a doubt, got more hectic than ever, and they leave us overwhelmed and overstimulated. Do you find yourself more and more craving the comfort of quiet spaces and calm environments? No wonder our brains process environmental stimuli differently when we are fatigued and stressed or struggling with mental health problems. By simply changing our environment, creating a comfortable space, and minimizing clutter, we can positively impact our mood, thoughts, and behaviors at home, in the classroom, or at the office.

To set the tone for my reflections, I want you to imagine a painting competition in which the participants were asked to create a picture titled "Peace." Many painters submitted their work, and after careful examination, the jury chose two finalists. One artist painted a perfectly calm lake, with gorgeous mountains slopes behind, sunny skies, and a reflection of birds and flowers in the water – pure tranquility. The second artist painted a very different picture: rocky mountain range, dark skies, very stormy weather, rapids with the water loudly tumbling down, and right underneath the waterfall, there was a small bush. In this bush, the mother bird made a nest, caring for her babies safely hiding under her wings.

Which one of the two pictures do you think has won?

Which one would you choose?

When you think about tranquility, what comes to mind?

What do you imagine thinking about peaceful, calm, and relaxing spaces?

Peace and tranquility can be perceived and experienced very differently. Whether it's a green meadow, a deserted wild beach, a beautiful lake, or a river lazily flowing on a warm sunny day, we find tranquility in natural outdoor environments. We can also create peace and tranquility in our indoor surroundings, living spaces, schools, and offices in a relatively simple way which helps make people feel calmer and less stressed.

Scientific studies show a direct correlation between specific environments and levels of relaxation, stress reduction, longevity, and pain relief. Here are seven simple tips on how to boost the tranquility of an area and create a calm space:

1. The first step is to reduce manufactured noise and introduce as many natural soothing sounds as possible. Different sounds can promote different moods. Having "natural" sounds can help to make a place feel more tranquil. We can achieve it by installing a water feature or a pond which will promote relaxation and encourage waterfowl and

other birds to visit. We can also play soothing background sounds of nature indoors, such as waves gently crashing on the beach, a waterfall, a tropical rain shower, or relaxing music.

2. The second idea to boost the tranquility of an area is to increase the number of natural features by planting trees, shrubs, and flower beds outdoors and placing live plants and flowers, which creates a green oasis indoors.

3. The third way to create a calm and tranquil space is by using the right colors; for best results, try choosing a color palette that works for you. For example, cool colors can be soothing and energizing, and colors found in nature can be grounding and peaceful.

4. Another idea is related to smells. Consider what smells are good for you and fill the space with aromas by using scented candles, aromatherapy, or cooking smells of your favorite comfort foods.

5. Yet another way to bring outdoorsy tranquility indoors is by using certain textures. You can recreate positive memories by surrounding yourself with things that make you feel good: wrap yourself in a comfortable blanket, put seashells on the bathroom counter, and fill

the bowl with pinecones or smooth stones from the outside.

6. Similarly, objects can also significantly impact the space you are in. Fill your space with things that lift your mood: photos of family and friends or favorite places, wildflowers, inspirational quotes, keepsakes, souvenirs from your trips, memorabilia, etc.

7. And finally, decluttering any space will help the positive energy flow and create calmness and tranquility. It goes for physical and virtual spaces; too much "stuff" can feel overwhelming. So, get rid of, donate, or sell things you don't need and don't use, clear your mailbox by unsubscribing from junk email, and get organized.

Ever since I was a child, I have loved to create small tranquil spaces in my house; I mimicked natural springs by putting colorful rocks I collected on various trips and placed them together with wildflowers in the dish filled with water. Later living on my own in an apartment, I had a small tabletop fountain that looked like a waterfall; I always had lots of natural plants: small palms, cactuses, yuccas, etc. Now living in a house surrounded by a garden, I built a koi pond and waterfall, which became a refuge for local birds like blue jays, robins, and cardinals. Next, I planted butterfly-attracting plants, and now I have a private oasis in my backyard. Inside my house, there is also balance and harmony. I use my favorite colors, burn scented candles and incense, use essential oils, and listen to soothing, relaxing music. I am surrounded by soft textures of blankets, pillows, and rugs. My home is my sanctuary where I can rest and rejuvenate.

There are countless other ways to increase the quality of your life by creating more peace and tranquility. So next time you feel stressed out, try to find a tranquil space or, even better, make one of your own – that way, you can get your little bit of calm anytime you want. It doesn't matter what environment you are in; you can always create a makeshift tranquil, and peaceful space that is as unique as you.

> **"If you can eliminate it, you'll have more time and more tranquility. So, ask yourself at every moment, is this necessary?"**
>
> **-Marcus Aurelius**

12

The Power
Of
Mental Preparation

*"Everything that you are going
through is preparing you for what you
asked for."*

It was an early Saturday morning, and as I was getting dressed, putting on my leggings, a sports bra, and a dry-fit shirt, and I was lacing my running shoes, in my head, I was quickly going through the checklist of everything I needed to take with me on my run: a hydration vest with water supply, couple small bottles with electrolytes, my watch with a tracking app, my cell phone, a change of clothes.

The day has come, I trained for it for many weeks, and I was about to participate in my first Half Marathon.

To say that running 13.1 miles (21 kilometers) was a big deal for me is an understatement because I have never run a distance this long. But I signed up for it feeling encouraged after completing 5k in June and 10k in December that year. So, I was officially in the game of running, but more importantly, I was also in the game of personal development.

When preparing for this race, I had to train and practice running, increasing my stamina and agility, but equally, if not, more importantly, I had to train my mindset and how I think. I vividly remember my mentors talking about the importance of mental preparation. For example, simple visualizing can dramatically increase the chance of succeeding in any given challenge. But not just the visualization of the outcome or the result (in my case, crossing the finish line and receiving the medal) but first and foremost, the whole process leading to it (envisioning running the entire course of the race, especially the final stretch when it gets tough). For me, the last two miles of the race were very challenging. Still, because I had already "experienced" it earlier in my head, I could focus on outside sensations and think of what I could see, smell, hear, and feel, and the struggle almost disappeared.

Another thing to remember is trying to imagine things not going on as planned ahead of time. If we could foresee some scenarios, situations, various obstacles, and roadblocks that we may find on our way, then if they happen, they won't surprise, shock, and disappoint us as much. We may even have the solution ready. For example, during my race, several things happened not according to plan: my watch, even though fully charged, died on me right at the first 500m (luckily, I was able to use a different tracking app on my phone), the water container started to leak and got me soaked and wet (there was not much I could do about it during the race, but afterward I changed to dry clothes).

And finally, having mental support from family and friends who will cheer you on is also incredibly important. Knowing that people believe in you is the best motivator.

**"Give me six hours to chop down
a tree and I will spend the first
four sharpening the axe."**

Abraham Lincoln

13

The Power
Of
The Willpower

*"In the absence of willpower, the most
complete collection of virtues and
talents is wholly worthless."*

-Aleister Crowley

Have you ever heard someone saying, "You can do it, just use your willpower"? Chances are you have; yes, willpower is considered one of the greatest human strengths. However, each of us has a certain amount of will available, and if not used properly, it can significantly drain or even totally deplete it.

Before we dig deeper into learning how to use willpower effectively, let us first define it. We can describe willpower in many ways, but some of the most common synonyms are drive, determination, self-discipline, self-control, self-regulation, and effortful control. At the core of willpower is the ability to resist short-term temptations and desires to achieve long-term goals. It's the dominant source of long-term satisfaction over instant gratification.

We rely on willpower to perform complex or demanding tasks, exercise, diet, save money, quit smoking, stop drinking, overcome procrastination, and ultimately accomplish any of our goals. It impacts every area of our lives. It is proven that people with more incredible willpower are happier, healthier, more satisfied in their relationships, wealthier and more advanced in their careers, and better able to manage stress, deal with conflict, and overcome adversity.

So how can we work in sync with willpower instead of against its nature?

The study of Positive Intelligence teaches us that the negative voices in our head, aka Saboteurs, push us to action based on negative emotions such as stress, frustration, anxiety, fear of failure or looking bad, etc.

This negative push of Saboteurs drains our reservoir of willpower, and as a result, the depleted willpower causes various consequences in different areas of life. For example, we can't resist temptations, become impatient with others, aren't resilient, and don't recover quickly from distress and failure.

On the other hand, the wiser part of our brain, also known as the Sage, pulls us into action through positive emotions like empathy, curiosity, wonder, creativity, passion, or compelling vision. This pull of the Sage based on positive emotions is effective and doesn't require willpower to keep going, it's easier, and it flows naturally. Using Sage's perspective and turning things into something more positive, something we want to do rather than must do, we are much more likely to accomplish our goals.

Shifting to pull instead of push means we keep our reservoir of willpower full so we can draw from it to be more patient with others, handle unexpected challenges standing in our way, and recover from failures faster.

So regardless of what we plan to achieve, we must make it more compelling and be a pull, not a push.

Here are a few ways to strengthen willpower: learning how to manage stress, setting small, achievable goals, and focusing on achieving them, planning, avoiding temptations, rewarding yourself, getting support, and finally, getting better sleep, exercise, meditation, and nutrition to manage the energy properly.

Willpower is like a muscle: The more you train it. The stronger it gets.

"Where there's a will, there's a way. Perhaps tomorrow, if not today."

-Michele Jennae

14

How To Become Your Version Of Roger Bannister

"The man who can drive himself further once the effort gets painful, is the man who will win"

-Sir Roger Bannister

"The Bannister Effect" is the phenomenon of one person showing others that it can be done and, thus, prompting others to believe and achieve.

In case you are not familiar with this famous story from the athletic world of runners, let me briefly remind you: On May 6th, 1954, Roger Bannister was the first to run one mile under 4 minutes, clocking in at 3 minutes and 59.4 seconds. By crushing the 4-minute mile mark, he broke the nine-year-old record and allowed runners to dream of the impossible. Before him, no one could do it, but afterward, many other people did it. His record lasted just 46 days. And even though some may point out that the tidy narrative of psychological breakthrough, unleashing the potential of humans to realize they too can run under 4 minutes, is false because the same phenomenon took place in other distances. Nevertheless, the fact that we can achieve amazing things in sports and other areas of our lives is undeniable.

Let me illustrate this with my examples in running and business.

I am a sprinter by nature; back in school, I was good at running the 100-meter dash and the 100-meter hurdles but running anything longer was quite challenging for me. Distances like the 5 km, 10 km, Half Marathon, or Marathon seemed unachievable.

During the pandemic, I began to fantasize about running longer distances. So, I started to challenge myself as I downloaded an app on my phone, which helped me take all the necessary steps to prepare myself—ultimately leading me to run in a 5 km race I tackled in the summer of 2020. Shortly after, I decided to try to conquer the 10 km, and again I started preparing by training and consistently increasing the distance by small increments. Finally, 14 weeks later, I completed the 10 km race beating my best record by 7 minutes. And I didn't stop there. I am pleased to report that I also ran and finished a Half Marathon, again without any crazy expectations regarding the time, just proving to myself that I can do anything I put my mind to.

Another example from my business is related to copywriting. English is not my native language, and I was always super insecure about writing even the shortest posts on social media. But, once again, in 2020, I decided to get out of my comfort zone, and after I got invited to participate in two collab book projects and write my chapters, even though skeptical, I agreed, and I did it. The fact that both books: "One" - Your wellness guide to body, mind, and soul as well as "#stayhome - when you can't go outside what happens on the inside…? became international bestsellers in multiple categories on Amazon astounded me, but more importantly, I started believing in my ability to write on a larger scale.

I am my version of Roger Bannister, and I know you can become one too.

So how do you do that? I'm glad you asked.

Here are the ten necessary steps:

- First, you need to want to achieve a specific goal.
- Next, you must make the decision that you are going to do it no matter what.
- Then it would help if you planned it
- Schedule it in your calendar.
- Begin without excuses and procrastination.
- Challenge yourself in the process.
- Get out of your comfort zone often.
- Break down the goal into manageable steps.
- Progress in small increments.
- And finally, and most importantly, never give up.

Anything is Possible! Really! ANYTHING!!!

"Just because they say it's impossible, doesn't mean you can't do it"

Sir Roger Bannister

15

When Crystals Call Your Name

"In a crystal we have clear evidence of the existence of a formative life principle, and though we cannot understand the life of a crystal, it is nonetheless a living being"

-Nicola Tesla

I always liked beautiful precious, and semi-precious stones, but in the past, I didn't call them crystals, and I didn't have any particular interest in learning about them, their origin, or their meaning.

I noticed, though, that particularly in the last couple of years, the crystals "found me." What I mean by that is either someone gifted me a necklace, pendant, or bracelet, or I stumbled upon a store selling unusual rocks in some foreign country and had to buy myself a souvenir.

Recently crystals entered my life in an even more significant way. For my first Full Moon Manifesting ritual, I purchased a few crystals. I found a local specialty shop and went on a crystal shopping spree. Beforehand I did a little research: I learned which ones are the most potent regarding the manifesting rituals and which have energy aligned with my Zodiac sign. Equipped with this knowledge, I began my experience. I knew that some of the crystals, like clear and rose quartz preferably, should have a point; the rest could be naturally shaped or tumbled.

I realized that visiting the store and being surrounded by all these beautiful colorful crystals made me feel amazing. I enjoyed touching them, holding them in my hands, and feeling their smooth surface. I made my first small purchase and was ready for the manifesting ritual.

But afterward, something unusual happened; I felt a powerful nudge and pull to return and get more of them. So I picked a different shop and felt terrific being amongst crystals again. I browsed around and got compelled to add a few more to my collection. The crystal that comes to us is the one we need now.

I learned how to correctly cleanse crystals, charge them, and enjoy their beauty.

I also started studying more and more about them. I found out about their unique energies and healing properties and learned more ways to use their power in manifestations.

On one particular New Year's Eve, I created my very first crystal grid. Crystal grids are potent energy tools used when manifesting dreams, goals, and intentions. Their power comes from the union of energies between the healing stones, sacred geometry, and the set meaning. The power of crystals in geometric patterns magnifies the intention to manifest results much faster.

Although we technically can't consider them alive organisms, Nikola Tesla said, "Crystals are living beings at the beginning of creation and as all things have energy and vibration." They have incredible power, balance the energies of an organism, and heal naturally by harmonizing the mind, body, emotions, and spirit. They can enhance learning, alleviate stress, uplift, calm, and energize. There is something magical about keeping them around.

And to me, they bring joy!

> **"Crystals amplify
> the consciousness."**
>
> **- Shirley MacLaine**

16

The Art
Of
Letting Go

*"Accept yourself, love yourself,
and keep moving forward. If you
want to fly, you have to give up what
weighs you down."*

Roy T. Bennett

Have you ever tried hard to make something happen, but no matter how much effort you put into it and how many different approaches you tested, it was not working? So, perhaps you stopped caring about it, or you gave up, and it happened at that exact moment! Whether or not you were aware, you detached yourself from the outcome. You let go!

Let me share my personal story as a powerful example of how life often works in mysterious ways. I was diagnosed with huge cysts on both ovaries as a young woman. When I found out about them, the doctor told me we must remove them asap, so I underwent surgery. Thankfully the procedure was successful, but afterward, I received the sad news that due to the size of the cysts, my ovaries were practically gone, and chances were that I wouldn't be able to have children in the future. This news hit me hard, and it only became more upsetting when I got involved in a steady relationship with my future husband. Fast forwarding, we had already been dating for a couple of years, and at this point, I gave up the idea of becoming a mommy. We decided to get married, and you guessed it, I got pregnant on our honeymoon. Nine months later, I gave birth to our amazing daughter, which was a medical miracle, and to top it off, four years later, I got pregnant again and gave birth to our wonderful son—another gift from heaven.

We must learn to let go to receive. Whether it's material objects, an experience, or an awareness, we must be willing to let go knowing it's a done deal. Letting go and surrendering to the Universe for the highest and best to be delivered to us.

Detachment from the outcome is also a matter of trust. This idea was and sometimes still is the hardest thing for me to comprehend. To fully surrender and trust that I am protected and that all the blessings will come to me in the divine timing can be very challenging. But the more I experience it; I realize that pushing for an outcome on my terms is just not how the Universe works

It is also true when it comes to manifesting. We first create a desire, then express it, and then we must let go with the conviction that it already happened. The moment we surrender the outcome is when the Universe can get to work. We must have a clear picture in our mind of what we want; we must believe without a shadow of a doubt that if it happened in our imagination, we must feel the energy of the outcome we desire, then the physical manifestation is sure to be.

We don't just say it.

We believe it.

And so it is.

"The greatest step towards a life of simplicity is to learn to let go.

-Steve Maraboli

17

Why Hard Work Doesn't Work

*"Hard work beats talent,
when talent doesn't work."*

There is a famous bronze statue on 5th Avenue in front of the Rockefeller Center in NYC - Atlas holding the Earth on his shoulders. It doesn't matter if you believe either the ancient Greek myth that Zeus enslaved Atlas to hold up the Earth on his shoulders for all eternity or the opposite version that envisions him holding up an entirely different celestial object, the sky). It seems like he is struggling.

Directly across the street in St Patrick's Cathedral, there is another sculpture; this one is of Jesus holding in his hand a small orb representing the World. Here Jesus is not straining or struggling; he is effortlessly holding the globe in his hand, radiating peace.

This metaphor reminds me of something I have been fascinated about in recent years: the hustle and grind vs. flow and ease in our daily lives. This topic is occupying my mind because the more conscious I get, the more I realize that loosening my grip on life will help me live more fully. I want to live life by my design and with my unique pace. It's not sustainable to push all the time or attempt to match the speed of everyone else but myself.

Let me share another metaphor. There are two entirely different sports disciplines on ice: hockey and curling. The objective of both games is to move either the pack or the stone across the ice. The methods of how both games work, however, are very different. In hockey, the puck is hit by the stick, usually very hard; in curling, there is no contact with the stone. Instead, the players "sweep" the ice with brooms to make them curl less and travel a greater distance.

Again, whether it's the hard-hitting, puck-flying action of hockey or the precision sliding and sweeping of curling, we can achieve similar outcomes very differently.

Hard work is mentally and physically exhausting, and it draws out the energy we need to maintain things that matter in life, like relationships with family and friends. How often do we work on an intensely physically or mentally draining project and find ourselves at the end of the day burnt out, exhausted, and too strung out to care about our loved ones? It's time to stop grasping things so tightly, holding on for dear life. Lightening up and approaching each day with more lightheartedness and willingness to have fun is ok. It's the "not" rushing, pushing, and trying hard to live that makes the life worth living. To feel alive, we need to allow more space for acceptance and balance; we must surrender and let go of control. It will bring a higher sense of inner peace, more freedom, and joy to our lives!

We all have a choice, we can continue to carry the World on our shoulders and struggle like Atlas, or we can surrender and give control of the World to higher powers: God, Universe, or Energy, whichever we believe in.

"The man on the top of the mountain didn't fall there"

-Vince Lombardi

18

How To Stop Deadly Consumption Syndrome

"When inspiration does not come to me, I go halfway to meet it."

-Sigmund Freud

Can you relate to this?

- You buy tons of books and build your "shelf-esteem" - they end up on the shelf, and you don't read them.

- You enroll in countless courses and begin but don't finish them.

- You attend various seminars and conferences and grab valuable insights but don't implement them.

- You listen to podcasts, read blogs, and feel like an imposter.

- You watch YouTube videos and tutorials and feel like you are not good enough to create your own.

- You purchase programs but never use them because you forgot about them.

When you are an entrepreneur, a business owner, and at the same time a lifetime learner, when you love reading, studying, and simply immersing yourself in the knowledge, there is a real danger of falling into the trap of "Consumption syndrome" nobody told you about.

I know this syndrome so well because I was an embodiment of it for years. I was enrolling in countless certification programs and attending in-person and online events, it seemed like they were multiplying in front of me, and my FOMO (Fear of missing out) was killing me. I was constantly chasing the next shiny object, the next thing I thought I needed to learn to succeed. And even though I completed many of the programs I purchased, over the years, the cost, both in time and money, started to approach a ridiculous number.

Until one day, I realized; this was insanity. The more I consumed, the less creative I became. I looked at my ideas from the past, and I could not believe that I had created so many amazing things, while at this point, I could not focus on making anything happen. Instead, my life felt just like an endless note-taking process. Maybe I learned a lot, but I often created very little of my original work. I realized I was addicted to consumption. My brain unconsciously slowed down the process of producing original ideas; instead, it recycled and produced a lower-quality remix of what I consumed. I was so engrossed in studying new subjects and absorbing brilliant new ideas and strategies that I forgot that life is not only about consuming other people's intellectual properties but, more importantly, about creating my own.

I learned from studying from different brilliant minds, mentors, and teachers that, yes, it is necessary to improve and get better at your craft constantly, but at the same time, not to fall into the trap of overconsuming. It is so easy to lose yourself in the sea of books, courses, blogs, podcasts, videos, etc., that days, weeks, and months can go by just consuming them all.

Consuming is always available, easy to access, it's always an option, and it becomes an autopilot activity. Unfortunately, the things we consume usually can't satisfy our hunger for more than a moment. While strategic consuming is a necessary element of learning and creating, we must be careful because while consuming content, we often multi-task or consume through different platforms at once, which makes it less effective.

Constant consumption also causes the devastating comparison game and, ultimately, the not-enoughness, an imposter syndrome, and stops us from creating anything of value.

If this sounds familiar, don't feel guilty. It is a natural path for many people at the beginning of their journey. The critical distinction here, though, is at the beginning! There must come a time when you say enough is enough, put the stake in the ground, and start creating.

You decide that you won't waste your life-consuming things anymore.

Instead of feeling empty and unfulfilled after mindless consumption, you begin feeling satisfied by creating something using your natural gifts in ways that are good for you and others. It is not easy to break off that consumption habit, but it is possible. And if I could do it, you can too.

What is the solution? How can we become more creative, produce original content, and stop deadly consumption? Here are some tangible tips you can apply right away:

- Boost your creativity by unplugging and connecting with nature, doing something you love, surrounding yourself with inspirational people and art, trying something new, creating a mood by listening to your favorite music, etc.

- Make consuming more difficult and accessible: delete or hide social media from your phone, change passwords often, etc.

- Make creating easier by focusing on and designating a particular time and place.

- Find the medium that you like, and that resonates with you.

- Write a post, a blog, or a book chapter instead of just reading someone else's.

- Shoot a video or go live instead of browsing YouTube.

- Make real connections with real people instead of wasting time with superficial "friends".

- Say "NO" more often to offers and proposals that don't serve you now.

Remember: Creativity sits in the absence of consumption.

"So, stop consuming!

- Create!"

19

Learning
From
Other
People's Mistakes

*"Only a fool learns from his own
mistakes. The wise man learns from
the mistakes of others"*

- Otto von Bismarck

Learning from other people's mistakes was something I always wanted to master. But, of course, I learned plenty from my missteps and oversights, and I knew there was no failure, only feedback, but the high achiever in me speculated that if I could only watch other people try and fail. I could then apply their learnings to my life, which would be even more powerful.

I often heard my mentors saying that they changed and transformed their lives after going through a crisis or living through a life-altering experience like bankruptcy, near-death accident, loss of a loved one, serious illness, etc.

In their hero's journey, they pointed out how they learned from these pivotal moments and the mistakes they made. As a result, they understood what they must change to transform their lives.

Learning from others' mistakes sometimes takes more work. I tried to imagine failing badly, hitting the proverbial wall or the very rock bottom, so I could act as if it happened and avoid potential failure. I tried to demonstrate courage as if I had no choice, and I had to act quickly as if my life depended on it. But I am not going to lie; even though it was possible to simulate specific scenarios, it was often hard to fool my mind that something dire had happened. My brain knew that there were other options open, and that's why it was hard to act as if I was dangling at the end of the rope.

However, in many cases, we could avoid mistakes if we indeed learned from the mistakes of others. As in Eleanor Roosevelt's quote:

> **"Learn from the mistakes of others. You can't live long enough to make them all yourself."**

In fact, according to a recent study by two researchers at Bristol University in England, we learn from our mistakes, but it turns out that we could learn even more from others' mistakes.

> **"A mistake you do not learn from is a mistake you will repeat."**

So how do we learn and benefit from the mistakes of others?

Here are reasons people make mistakes in the first place:

1. The most critical initial reasons people fail are lack of preparation, poor planning, poor diagnosis of the problem, weak information, improper incentive, and inadequate resources.

2. Secondary reasons people fail are lack of focus, knowledge or experience, incorrect strategy, and poor execution.

3. The third group of reasons includes wrong assumptions, no sense of urgency, short-term mentality, careless behavior, poor attitude, ego or greed, avoidance or denial, and conflicting goals.

4. Finally, the crucial reason for failure is quitting before completion.

And here are ideas on how to turn mistakes into valuable lessons, ensuring that they won't happen again:

- Observe, take notes, and learn why and how people failed; you'll learn a lot.

- Don't try to figure everything out yourself; consider what others have done before and apply it.

- Try to avoid repeating mistakes, and keep tracking them.

- Share with others what you learn from mistakes made by other people.

- Don't blame yourself and others for the mistakes made; move on.

- Apply lessons learned from mistakes made in one area to another.

- Be patient, trying to figure out how to avoid the most common errors in the future.

- Visualize yourself in the situation and make better choices.

- Do some research on how others avoid making mistakes.

- And finally, have a mentality that there is no failure, only feedback- celebrate that!

Everyone makes mistakes at some point in life, but let's remember that when we make a mistake, we might be helping someone else avoid making the same mistake and learn from our failure!

So, I conclude with the quote by Anurag Prakash Ray:

"Everyone evolves by making mistakes and actually learning from them."

20

Work hard,
Relax Harder

"Smile, breathe, and go slowly."
-Thích Nhất Hạnh

101 Self-Care Ideas

Self-care is the highest form of self-love. I generally take good care of myself, but sometimes when I worked intensely on multiple complex projects, I noticed that I had come close to a dangerous state of burnout. Yes, it can happen to all of us.

The trick is recognizing and taking appropriate action before it is too late. I notice alarming signs, and I immediately go into protective mode. I double up on my self-care routines and rituals. And within just one three-day weekend, I can rejuvenate my body, mind, and soul and restore my physical and mental energy.

One recent event triggered me to brainstorm and create a list of 101 self-care activities I share below. Some are super simple; some require preparation, some you can do at home, and some need you to visit a specific location. Whatever you choose, try and enjoy a few or every single one of them if you feel like it.

In no particular order, here are the 101 ideas for self-care rituals you can start implementing right away:

1. Get a pedicure and a manicure.

2. Get a massage and facial

3. Read a book or a favorite magazine.

4. Sit in a garden or a backyard and listen to the birds singing or other sounds of nature.

5. Take a bubble bath with candles, essential oils, and relaxing music.

6. Pick or buy a bouquet of fresh flowers.

7. Go for a walk listening to your favorite music or sounds of nature.

8. Put on a homemade face mask.

9. Permit yourself to watch a Netflix show without guilt.

10. Take a nap without an alarm clock.

11. Order your favorite dinner.

12. Do something crafty: like creating a vision board or a crystal grid.

13. Go to the library or bookstore, find a quiet corner, and read.

14. Watch a funny movie and laugh hard.

15. Walk barefoot on the grass wet with the morning dew drops

16. Perform a new or full moon manifesting ritual

17. Take a dance lesson.

18. Take a day/week off from social media

19. Burn your favorite candle or diffuse some oils with scents you love

20. Sit in a coffee shop and enjoy a beautiful cup of coffee, not in a paper cup.

21. Go shopping at a fancy specialty grocery store and buy some delicious rare or exotic food.

22. Try out a new hobby.

23. Practice yoga.

24. Enjoy guided meditation.

25. Make a quiet and not rushed breakfast

26. Go for a ride in the car with the windows down and an open roof.

27. Go for a bike ride.

28. Go hiking.

29. Go to the beach.

30. Listen to your favorite podcast.

31. Have a 20-minute stretching or tapping session.

32. Go to the park, and people watch

33. Go swimming.

34. Plan your dream vacation or a weekend getaway.

35. Carefully dress up in clothes that make you feel great.

36. Declutter an area in your house or apartment.

37. Do something that you have been procrastinating on.

38. Bake cookies or a cake you love and eat some guilt-free

39. Watch the sunrise or sunset.

40. Have a picnic with a traditional basket, wine bottle, and sandwiches.

41. Go to bed early or sleep in late.

42. Research something and write an article about it.

43. Unfollow a bunch of people on your social media who don't add value to your life

44. Go to an art museum.

45. Go to a happy hour at a bar and enjoy a beautiful fancy cocktail/mocktail.

46. Buy yourself some new makeup.

47. Go to a sauna.

48. Take a nap outside on a hammock or a lounge chair.

49. Slowly and lovingly brush your hair with a luxurious brush.

50. Take the time to do your makeup and blow-dry your hair

51. Write a list of 10 things you are grateful for.

52. Prepare some healthy meals and snacks for the entire week.

53. Buy yourself a beautiful new journal or a book.

54. Call, write a letter, or email an old friend.

55. Cook your favorite meal and serve it in beautiful china.

56. Say "no" to someone.

57. Make your bed in the morning

58. Create a list of all your successes and accomplishments in life.

59. Refill your water bottle frequently.

60. Watch a TED talk or a motivational webinar.

61. Be selfish- prioritize yourself.

62. Write a list of things you love about yourself

63. Put your phone on do not disturb or airplane mode for a day

64. Buy a new mattress, or a pillow, or a set of new sheets

65. Change your sheets.

66. Try a new baking or cooking recipe.

67. Rearrange the furniture or redecorate some living spaces in your house

68. Create playlists for workouts, relaxing, meditating, creating, etc.

69. Look at positive affirmations and motivational quotes.

70. Watch videos of cute baby animals.

71. Organize your photos in albums and delete multiple pictures from your camera roll.

72. Just for fun, play an old phone game.

73. Organize your pantry or/and kitchen.

74. Cuddle in the softest clothes under the coziest blanket.

75. Start journaling.

76. Try a new calming and grounding breathing technique.

77. Learn something new.

78. Watch your favorite movie with friends, popcorn, and favorite drinks.

79. Go skiing or ice skating.

80. Do something nice for someone else.

81. Surprise a friend or a loved one.

82. Make a super healthy and delicious lunch and focus on chewing every bite.

83. Create a list of all the compliments people tell you.

84. Do absolutely nothing.

85. Sit by the fire pit.

86. Take a hot shower and ice bath.

87. Cuddle with a pet.

88. Take some great photos of yourself or nature.

89. Stare at the night sky full of stars.

90. Be a tourist in your city.

91. Sing Karaoke.

92. Solve a crossword puzzle.

93. Play your favorite board game with friends or family.

94. Read or write poetry.

95. Pray and or attend a religious ritual.

96. Participate in a book club.

97. Have a lunch date with a friend.

98. Get a coloring book and color like a kid.

99. Do something unexpected and spontaneous.

100. Start learning the basics of a new language.

101. Learn how to play an instrument.

Additionally, my best ideas and most valuable and brilliant insights come to me when I am in the shower, walk outside, and exercise. A massive benefit of self-love and self-care is better mental health because people who love and care for themselves are less likely to suffer from depression, anxiety, or low self-esteem. Self-love and self-care are so important because they impact a positive mindset essential for success in life and mental happiness.

So, schedule your personal "me time" in the calendar! You are worth it.

"Almost everything will work again if you unplug it for a few minutes, including you."

-Anne Lamott

21

How To 10X Your Energy And Vitality

*"The energy of the mind is
the essence of life."*

-Aristotle

How energetic you are is closely related to your success in life. Having more vitality means being physically able to do more in life, having the desire to take action, the drive to try new things, and the mental and emotional vigor. High energy leads to purpose, surviving change, finding joy in everyday life, and being in top shape. The good news is there are multiple ways to boost your energy. Below I am describing three of them.

Three proven ways to boost your energy:

1. Increase strength and endurance:

If you haven't started exercising yet, now is the time. Physical vitality is the foundation of everything that comes as a result. The moment you start moving your body is the moment you build momentum and thus fuel your brain. After exercising, you're more likely to act on your goals.

2. Think clearly:

The best way to boost your energy is to focus on mental vitality, which is the ability to think clearly. As a result, you'll make better decisions; you will control what goes on in your mind; you will be able to turn negative into positive and let your creativity out. To encourage better thinking and train your brain, you can do the following: get enough sleep, learn new things, journal, brainstorm ideas, play mind games, avoid sugar, improve your memory, engage in new activities, learn a foreign language, interact with new people, get better at problem-solving, meditate, take breaks often when doing focused work, hydrate (dehydration is one of the main reasons for brain fog), weaken your bad memories, learn more about analytical thinking.

3. Raise your happiness levels:

The third aspect of vitality is emotional. So, to boost your energy and be more successful, you'll need to feel better, be positive, and be at peace. Start by decluttering your life. Stop spending time with toxic people. Stop doing things you don't feel like doing and which make you miserable. Get rid of possessions you aren't using. Ditch the stress by leaving behind negative thoughts, anxiety, and bad habits you've developed over the years.

Then start taking better care of your emotional health and spirituality. Welcome mindfulness in your life, and do things slowly. Enjoy any activity more by being present and accepting it's the best you could be doing now. Such an attitude of appreciation will make you more grateful and happier as a result.

Vitality is a life force; it's the foundation of being filled with energy and making the most of your days.

Make sure you pay attention to all three areas of vitality - the physical, mental and emotional.

Take small actions daily to boost your energy, and you will see progress in all fields.

Below I share more tips on increasing your overall energy and vitality.

Energy-generating ideas:

Regardless of age, we can experience low energy, fatigue, and exhaustion in every stage of our life. If you wake up tired every day, you are not alone. Healthy habits are the key to maintaining a satisfying quality of life. A healthy day-to-day routine enables you to boost energy and handle the inevitable physical changes of aging.

Here are the ten most critical habits you should adopt for more energy and vitality:

1. Be mentally active
2. Practice energy-generating exercises
3. Don't smoke
4. Eat high-protein foods
5. Get plenty of sleep
6. Get the right vitamins and nutrients
7. Nourish your spirit with meaningful activities
8. Practice healthy stress management
9. Stay hydrated
10. Stay socially connected.

"The power plant doesn't have the energy; it generates it"
– Brendon Burchard

Energy is a decision we must make and not something we have. Every day we can generate as much energy as we want using different methods and techniques.

It is very different for everyone, and everyone must find out what works best for them. Perhaps it is meditation, yoga, or other types of exercise, or maybe it is the conviction that energy-generating every day is necessary.

Energy is everything.

Work on increasing your energy by using proven methods.

How to increase your energy in the morning:

1. Quality sleep is one of the best ways to ensure energy the next day; enough hours of sleep will boost it quicker than you think. So go to sleep and wake at the same time, if possible, and sleep at least 7 hours every night (optimally 8-9 hours). And if you don't get enough sleep at night, try at least to take a 15-minute power nap.

2. Drinking water helps your body perform at its highest potential all day. Warm lemon water first in the morning kicks off your digestive system and starts energizing your whole body. It helps purify your liver, boosts your metabolism, improves your immune and cardiovascular system, helps with heartburn and constipation, freshens your breath, and increases your energy.

3. Stretching first thing in the morning - stretch out your whole body as soon as you wake up. It will shake off morning laziness, get your blood flowing, release any stiffness and kinks that may have developed during the night, and leave you limber and invigorated to tackle your day.

4. Don't hit snooze because it sucks away energy for the rest of the day. Hitting the snooze button makes it harder to wake up and affects your energy levels all day long. A more consistent wake-up time will help you skip the snooze button and wake up naturally with more energy.

How to increase your energy during the day:

5. Drink tons of water daily - water is essential to your health and weight management. General recommendations are ½ oz of water

for every pound of your body weight, up to 100 oz. Don't forget that the standard glass is 8oz. So, for example, a 130 pounds person needs to drink 65 ounces (8 glasses) of water per day.

6. Exercise regularly every day or at least 3-4 times per week. Work on your strength and endurance because this will increase your energy. A morning workout triggers feel-good endorphins and lowers elevated stress hormones. Effects can last 6-8 hours.

7. Eat high-fiber, low-glycemic foods. Vegetables, the number one energy-boosting food, should make up a third of your diet. They prevent you from feeling hungry too soon and prevent highs and lows in blood sugar. Fruits are great, too but try to eat only a few high-sugar varieties, such as watermelon, cantaloupe, and mangoes.

8. Declutter your workspace. When your desk or inbox looks like a war zone, you feel stressed out. Please take a few minutes daily to clean up and get organized, so it doesn't feel so overwhelming later. A calmer, more Zen work environment keeps you feeling "on," connected, and productive.

9. Instead of second coffee in the afternoon, drink herbal teas full of antioxidants such as peppermint, chamomile, nettle, sage, or regular green tea. Green tea works as an antidepressant, improve blood flow, lowers cholesterol, helps prevent a range of heart-related issues, helps keep blood sugar stable, may help destroy cancer cells, and helps slow down and relax.

10. You can gain energy by going for a half-hour walk outside; if you can't do 30 minutes, do at least a 15-minute walk, rain or shine, primarily if you work all day behind the desk. The fresh air and brisk walk will energize you and sharpen your focus on your "to-do" list.

11. Laugh! Even if it's hard! Laugh at yourself, laugh at a funny movie, remember funny times, and laugh again. Laughter releases good endorphins into your brain, making you feel good and giving you more energy. There is a good reason why there is a saying: "Laughter is health."

12. Every day, set aside some quiet time - a key to restoring and maintaining vitality is becoming conscious of your present thinking patterns and choices and how they may affect your health. Clear your mind of

all the accumulated debris and clutter from technology and media, to-do lists, and negative thoughts. Concentrate on positive aspects of life and repeat positive self-talk mantras. Relax by listening to music, taking a bath, or a nap (but not after 6 pm)

13. Don't schedule too many things in one day. Some days are going to be busy, but if every single day you have too many things on your to-do list, you will find yourself drained of energy before you even start your day. Check your schedule and lighten it up for a while. Focus on the essential must-do tasks.

14. Stay away from energy vampires - An energy vampire is a person who feeds off your emotional or psychic energy. These individuals generally lack empathy, sensitivity, and emotional maturity. As a result of the pain or insecurity they feel inside, energy vampires are preying on the vitality of others in an attempt to heal their inner suffering.

15. Work on your self-worth and self-esteem. A low level or lack of these will drain your energy, and make you feel sad, ashamed, insecure, overly self-critical, and worthless, which can lead, in effect, even to depression. Self-esteem leans towards doing, vs. Self-worth is more

about being. Both serve different purposes in life and work beautifully together.

16. Your posture can affect your mood and energy. Walking with a slouched posture can lead to feelings of depression or decreased energy. You can reverse these feelings by walking in a more upright position; it can improve mood and energy levels. It is very similar to the principle "Fake it till you make it" - you can convince your body that you have more energy.

How to increase your energy in the evening:

17. Skip the night cup - After a long day, a few glasses of wine or a nice cocktail might seem like a perfect way to unwind, but alcohol can disrupt your natural sleep cycle and leave you exhausted the following morning. If you are dealing with energy issues, it's best to say no to alcohol before bed.

18. Detox your home - All the chemicals we're exposed to inside our home can drain our energy. We can find toxic substances in household cleaning products, cosmetics, nonstick cookware, plastic food storage containers, and manufactured goods. Replace all these items throughout your home with healthy natural alternatives.

19. Eliminate the use of electronics before bed - Turn off all the screens one or two hours before sleep. Instead of TV, cell phone, computer, tablet, or electronic game, wind down with an article or book. This change seems small but makes an enormous difference. If you keep your electronics on all night, it affects your demeanor the following morning.

20. Having sex. Getting your sex life up and running is essential for vital energy flow. What's more, it creates a virtuous cycle - the healthier and more energetic you feel, the stronger your libido gets. The stronger your sex drive, the more often you'll enjoy lovemaking. Recharging your sexual energy is good for overall health.

Supplements and natural energy boosters:

1. Ginseng - used for centuries to strengthen the body- contains compounds that can help overcome stress by supporting adrenal glands' hormone production. It also increases mental alertness and energy, enhances one's sense of well-being, and boosts sex drive.

2. Rhodiola - this potent herb is used to boost physical endurance, energy, and moods and heighten mental clarity, sexuality, and speed

recovery after exercise. In addition, it assists in adapting to stress which prevents adrenal fatigue and supports the thyroid gland.

3. Essential oils - it's true that certain smells like Peppermint, Wild Orange, and Rosemary can give you energy. Even when applying aromatherapy massage, using one of these oils can help you increase your overall energy.

4. Reishi - contains compounds with numerous health-enhancing effects, including adrenal gland support. In addition, it has a cumulative beneficial effect on your kidneys, stimulating your sexual energy and overall vitality.

5. Vitamin C - when you go through acute or chronic stress, you can lose a lot of vitamin C through your urine and may experience stress-induced adrenal fatigue. Vitamin C helps the body produce adrenal hormones.

6. Vitamin B5 - also known as Pantothenic acid, plays a crucial role in your body's production of adrenal hormones. Use it for adrenal fatigue due to stress. You can get it from whole grains, legumes, broccoli, cauliflower, salmon, sweet potatoes, and tomatoes.

And finally, by far my favorite method of boosting energy

Vacations and other getaways - Everyone knows why holidays are great - they're fun! You don't have to work! But there are some surprising side benefits of traveling. It also can boost your wellness; help you be more energized and more productive:

- Vacations can cut your risk of heart attack

- Vacations boost your energy levels

- Vacations can help you get a raise

- Vacation adventures give you a natural high

- Vacations make you happier with your entire life

- Vacations can help the economy

- Vacations help keep your mind calm

- Vacation happiness is contagious

- Vacation may help you live a longer and happier life

- Vacations force you to improve your workflow.

**"The world belongs
to the energetic"**

– Ralf Waldo Emerson

22

How to
De-Clutter
Your Life

*"De-clutter your mind, your heart,
your home. Let go of the heaviness
that is weighing you down, make your
life simple but significant".*

– Unknown

If you are reading these words, chances are that it is not a coincidence. Most of us could use some de-cluttering in our lives. And I don't mean just spring cleaning; I mean severe de-cluttering in all areas of our lives.

Here are a few questions you can ask yourself when in doubt if you should keep something or get rid of it:

1. Do you use it regularly?

2. Does it have sentimental value?

3. Do you save it "just in case"?

4. Do you have more than one?

5. Can something else replace it?

6. Do you love it?

7. Is it functional or beautiful?

8. Did you choose to bring it into your life?

9. Would it be hard to replace it?

10. Do you need to save it for tax or legal reasons?

11. If you were free from guilt, would you keep it?

12. Have you used it in the last year or past five years?

13. Does it fit your vision for the life you want to live?

Answer these questions and work on de-cluttering both physical and mental debris from your life. Today is your day to let go of things that no longer serve you and try to keep nothing in the house that you do not know to be useful or believe to be beautiful. Your home is your haven. You should feel relaxed the minute that you walk through your door. If you aren't feeling it, you need to make changes. How much time are you worrying about your clutter instead of living? Free yourself and get on with your life.

> **"Clutter is not just the stuff on the floor; it's anything that stands between you and the life you want to be living."**
>
> **– Peter Walsh**

We must look at de-cluttering in all areas of our lives: physical clutter, mental clutter, digital clutter, and finally, daily life clutter.

Physical clutter- "The more things you own, the more they own you" – Unknown. It is possible to de-clutter your material belongings in just 31 days. Depending on the size of your house, closets, and possessions, some categories can take you days, weeks, and even months. Here are the areas that we can focus on one by one when trying to eliminate things that no longer serve us:

- Fridge
- Pantry (Get rid of anything expired)
- Kitchen appliances/cookbooks
- Tupperware/kitchen storage
- Jewelry
- Movies and CDs
- Linen closet
- Kids closets
- Bathrooms
- Medicine cabinet
- Paperwork (Old receipts, bills, invoices)
- Toys
- Christmas stuff
- Stuffed animals
- Books and games
- Clothes (separate by season, keep, toss or donate))
- Shoes
- Accessories (Scarves, gloves, purses, belts)
- Outside/winter clothing
- Makeup/personal hygiene
- Apps on the phone

- Storage on computer
- The camera roll on the phone
- Photographs and memorabilia
- Attic
- Garage
- Car
- Home office and desk space (files, pens, organizers)
- Your purse
- Gadgets
- Souvenirs and chachkas

Mental clutter- "Clutter isn't just in your home, attic, garage, or office. Clutter is also in your mind and distracts you ". Here are eight ways to de-clutter your mind:

- Accept what is
- Be kind to yourself
- Release your guilt and fears
- Let go of control
- Visualize what's important
- Focus on your energy
- Allow yourself to be vulnerable

- Find what doesn't serve or interest you and let it go

Digital Clutter- "Clutter is nothing more than postponed decisions" – Unknown. This clutter is sneaky because it is less visible, and we know that what's out of sight it's out of mind. But if our electronic devices: phones, and computers, are cluttered, it not only slows our productivity and makes our communication inefficient but also drains our precious energy. So, here are a few ideas on how to de-clutter your digital devices:

- Make an audit and organize and get rid of duplicate files

- Back up everything stored digitally (cloud storage)

- Delete old programs and apps

- Clean up your mailbox – delete old emails

- Delete old text threads

- Go digital when possible (Autopay, paperless bills, e-statements)

**"Outer order contributes
to inner calm"**

–Gretchen Robin.

Daily Life Clutter- Our habits, routines, relationships, and social commitments also can be de-cluttered. If something is adding stress and not contributing to your well-being, eliminate it. Here are a few ideas:

- Conduct your calendar audit – say no more often

- Get a planner and create a planning system that works for you.

- Be clear on your short-term and long-term goals and prioritize and set SMART goals and action items.

And finally, for extra credit, you can take the Minimalist route; here are some ideas:

- Stop buying the unnecessary

- Toss half of your stuff

- Learn contentedness

- Reduce half again

- List 4 essential things in your life. Do these first; stop doing the non-essential

- Clear distractions focus on each moment

- Let go of attachment to doing, have more

- Fall in love with less.

To conclude, I will leave you with this thought by Peter Walsh:

> **"What I know for sure is that when you de-clutter, whether it's your home, your head, or your heart. It is astounding what will flow into that space that will enrich you, your life, and your family."**

23

Top Secrets
Of
Longevity

*"Don't live the same year
75 times and call it a life"*

-Robin Sharma

To live a long, happy, healthy life, possess vitality, and look youthful are ultimate goals for many people. So much is written on topic of reaching longevity while still being physically and mentally fit, and there is a lot of data on what one should do regularly to stay young and feel vibrant and energetic until old age.

According to the research, there are several areas where we can improve our behaviors and habits to promote long, happy, and healthy lives. Some ideas are simple, and logical, and some are more challenging and counterintuitive. Dr. John Demartini, a human behavioral specialist, offers an extensive list of ideas for, as he calls it, the expression of immortality.

Here are a dozen of excellent ideas:

1. Have a purpose and mission in life. People who know their purpose well and have a long-term vision for their lives live more vital and happier lives. As in the saying, "Without vision, the people perish", having a 100-year idea will keep you active and sharp in your 60s, 70s, 80s, and beyond.

2. Determine your values and make sure you live congruent with the highest ones. You must also align your goals with your values, ensuring you'll live by your design.

3. Keep your mind sharp. Continuously learn and teach others what you know. Stimulate your mind and keep it alert- practice brain exercises. Meditate to reach a state of gratitude and appreciation.

4. Keep your body active and flexible. Walk, stretch, swim, practice yoga, dance, have sex, etc. When your muscles are tight, and your body is rigid, you do not only feel old, but your mind is also not working to its fullest potential.

5. Eat quality foods. Chew your food well and consume fewer calories and less variety. Less stimulation from various types of foods reduces overeating. Don't eat late at night, and don't go to bed with a full stomach.

6. Hydrate your body by drinking plenty of water. Your muscles, joints, and all organs need water to function optimally. Coffee, tea, and juices don't count – drink them in moderation or eliminate them.

7. Rest and sleep adequately. If you love what you do and do what you love, you can't wait to get up from bed to do it. But you must sleep to recharge and revitalize your mind and body. Some people need 7 or 8 hours of sleep, some less.

8. Manage your emotions. Don't get too high or too low - keep your emotions balanced and your mind calibrated well. Proper breathing helps keep you centered and grounded. Breathe slow deep diaphragmatic breaths.

9. Socialize with people and hug them a lot. Don't sit in a chair and get old, be involved in society and interact; the more people you meet, the longer you'll live. Associate and spend time with youth.

10. Stop blaming and shaming yourself. Shame and guilt shorten your life. It's not about what happened to you but how it served your life, what you learned from, or what you could be grateful for.

11. Surround yourself with music you love. Collect music that brings tears of appreciation to your eyes and which inspires you. Inspired life keeps you youthful.

12. Take advantage of technologies and cosmetics that can give you a look of youthfulness. Take care of your skin, hair, nails, etc. You don't have to be afraid of aging, but you can maintain a healthy and youthful appearance.

Besides hard-core scientific research and studies that promote longevity, there are secrets and home recipes shared through generations by people who enjoyed long and happy lives.

Here are a few of those:

1. Drink wine at lunch
2. Go with the flow
3. Find a perfect partner
4. Drink many cups of tea
5. Eat ice cream
6. Don't stay in the sun too much
7. Don't squint
8. Don't forget to smile
9. Practice foreignness
10. Practice gratitude and appreciation
11. Think happily and have a youthful spirit
12. Have a sense of humor
13. Declutter your life
14. Eliminate toxic relationships.
15. Be optimistic
16. Eat blueberries

Try some of these tips and ideas and see if you can add more life to your years and more years to your life.

**"To sustain longevity,
You have to evolve"**

-Aries Spears

Epilogue

In this book, I covered many topics I am fascinated about, which, if applied, could significantly improve quality of life. Knowing your purpose is the singular most important thing to get unstuck and become unstoppable.

It is my true honor and the greatest pleasure to invite you to my one-of-a-kind workshop: "Discover your purpose and learn how to monetize it" where I will pull the curtain and share my proven, transferrable and sustainable 3 D Method: DEFINE your true purpose with a clarity you never knew before, DESIGN your exceptional life of fulfillment, freedom, and joy on your terms while creating a legacy, and DELIVER that purpose to the world monetizing it. It could be the best gift you could give yourself.

So as an implementation tool – please join my FREE workshop and you will learn tools and techniques to identify your purpose and monetize it.

Register for the FREE workshop "Discover your life's purpose and learn how to monetize it" by simply scanning the QR code below:

My Gifts For The Readers
Please scan this QR code to get
access to my gifts:

About me- Excerpts from an Exclusive Interview

Award-Winning Mentor, Keynote Speaker, two times International Best-Selling Author of "One"- Your wellness guide to body, mind, and soul and "#Stayhome"- When you can't go outside, what happens inside, Certified High Performance Coach™,

Certified Positive Intelligence Coach™, NLP and Time Line Therapy® Practitioner, Strategic Interventions Life Coach, Founder and CEO of "Coaching Journey with Jola" LLC, Wife, and Mother.

Introduce yourself! Please tell us about you and your life, so we can get to know you better.

I often call myself Travelholic and Personal Development Junkie. Although I love to travel and need it like I need oxygen to live, I also love all aspects of personal development. My other hobbies include foreign languages (besides my native Polish, I speak English, German and Russian), interior decorating, photography, and dance.

I was born and raised in Poland, where I completed my education with a master's degree in Scientific-Technical Information from Silesian University in Katowice. Last three decades, I have resided in the United States, where I started my own family. I have over 30 years of combined experience working with thousands of unique individuals and groups of people serving them in many different capacities. First, as a tour guide traveling worldwide (almost 70 countries visited so far) and translating into four languages, then working in the entertainment and hospitality industry as part of operational management in a large publicly traded company in NYC. Finally, coaching people initially as a fitness, wellness, and lifestyle coach and most recently more holistically as Certified High Performance Coach™, NLP and Time Line Therapy®, Practitioner, Certified Positive Intelligence Coach™, and Strategic Interventions Life Coach. I have been married for 26 years to an amazing, very supportive, and loving husband, Bill, and I am also a mom of two exceptional and very talented kids. My daughter Nicolette is a ballerina, and my son Chris is a lacrosse player. And here are a few FUN FACTS about me: I love adrenaline: I skydived in New York, scuba-dived in Hawaii, Zip-lined in Costa Rica, and even traveled to North Korea. I am a first-time pet owner; my children tricked me into adopting a puggle Jetty and couple of bunnies Oreo and Ol'Mo. I have Interior Decorating License. I love taking pictures, and on my camera roll alone, I have over 220000 photos.

What is your business name, and how do you help your clients?

I am a Founder and CEO of "Coaching Journey with Jola" LLC. I started my company four years ago, and as a coach, I am passionate about challenging my clients to discover their purpose and reach their highest potential. I have a proven ability to help them achieve transformational results. My direct coaching style is a perfect blend of fun, compassion, tough questions, bold challenges, and various tools from different coaching modalities. It allows me to get my clients desired outcomes and help them move from where they're at to where they want to be. I offer three types of coaching services: individual one-on-one sessions, coaching in small intimate group settings, and coaching retreats in exotic destinations worldwide. This last modality is my signature program, and it's my favorite because it marries my two biggest passions for travel and personal development.

My mission is to help one million women live to the fullest. Reach heightened and sustained levels of clarity, energy, courage, productivity, and influence and show them that it is possible to live lives of their dreams, on their terms, without regrets, be fully engaged, joyful and confident and build an incredible legacy.

What kind of audience do you target your business towards?

I empower executive women to DEFINE, DESIGN, AND DELIVER the life of fulfillment, joy, and purpose they genuinely yearn for using their untapped feminine potential. I help them to map out and create a life of freedom on their terms with no regrets, building a meaningful legacy. I help women who know that they have a greater purpose, but being in the comfort zone of their career, they feel unable to act on it. Even though they like their jobs and are good at what they do, it feels like it's not enough. They wake up every morning knowing they are meant for something greater, but their self-imposed limitations stop them. Some love what they do professionally but want to contribute more and have a more significant impact. And some of them grow tired of their careers because they feel dead inside.

What are your goals for your business?

I dedicated my life to understanding human behaviors, gaining clarity, and discovering true purpose and values relative to personal and business growth. I simplified the inner game of happiness and enabled crucial mindset shifts. With my proven proprietary 3D METHOD, I help executive women design and create the path to living the lives of purpose they yearn for. They can DEFINE their purpose that will fulfill them most, DESIGN the exact steps and systematic process to follow, and DELIVER their lives of meaning and contribution by following these steps. As a result, they get crystal clear clarity of what truly matters to them, and finally, they live their lives to the fullest, congruent, and aligned with their mission. My clients excel both personally and professionally.

Tell us about a pivotal moment that brought you to where you are today.

I started my journey with a personal breakthrough. For most of my life, I was very fit and slim and never had to worry about dieting or working out. Six years ago, I noticed my metabolism slowed, and I started putting on extra pounds. I not only disliked how I looked and how uncomfortable I felt in my skin, but I also realized that if I didn't stop this madness, I could get very sick. After my dream trip to Dubai and Abu Dhabi, I could not tolerate looking at myself in my pictures. I decided, "enough is enough" I changed my eating habits and started working out regularly; in 5 months, I shed 38 pounds, and on my 20th wedding anniversary, I could fit in my wedding gown. My transformation inspired many women; I decided to pass forward what I learned and became a fitness and wellness coach. My coach introduced me to High Performance, and I got hooked. In the process, I realized that even though my life looked picture-perfect on the outside, I had a missing piece in my heart; I wanted to live a more purposeful life and create a lasting legacy for my children. So, I started studying and skilling up. Fast-forwarding to today, I got certifications in multiple caching modalities. I started my business, "Coaching Journey with Jola" LLC, and I love helping people transform their lives holistically.

In the beginning, I lacked confidence; I had no idea how powerful my knowledge, expertise, and life experience were. But after using everything I learned in the past four decades, I created powerful and very effective systems and tools to empower women to move from living their lives in default to living and enjoying dream lives by design.

What are your plans for the near future?

I plan to grow and scale my online membership called "Exceptional Life Academy 2.0" – How to holistically up-level your life, a perfect blend of coaching, mentoring, teaching, and Q&As.

After a couple of years of uncertainty, I am ready to conduct coaching retreats again in exotic places around the globe. Super excited to be able to travel again.

And lastly, I am about to take my speaking and closing skills to the next level and become a Certified Closing Professional. I want to share my message with people online and offline on stages worldwide. I am embracing my feminine energy and living proof that anything is possible.

For more information, visit my websites:

www.coachingjourneywithjola.com
www.coachjola.com

ACKNOWLEDGMENTS

My Family:

My Husband Bill and my kids Nicolette and Chris

My coaches and mentors:

Brendon Burchard, Joel Bauer, Eben Pagan, Annie Lalla, Shirzad Chamine, Tony Robbins, Dean Graziosi, Lenka Lutonska, Mel Robbins, Marie Forleo, Rachel Hollis, John Assaraf, John, Demartini, Anand Rao, Paul O'Mahony, Robin Sharma, Sheri Rosenthal, Sajen Thathiah, Jake Davey, Jason Osborn, Wendy Maynard, Scott Jackson, Autumn Calabrese, Le Brown, Natalie Ledwell, Shanda Sumpter, Chloe Madanes, James Mel, Vito LaFata, Zeke Derilius, Sharan Sammi, Skip Archimedes, Maric Diamond, Vishen Lakhiani, Marie Kondo, Sarah Prout.

My publisher and the book coach:

Mirav Tarkka

Made in the USA
Middletown, DE
22 January 2023

22044542R00089